QUIT YOUR SMOKING HABITS

Kay D Johnson

Johnson, Kay D
Quit Your Smoking Habits

ISBN 978-1989194959 (pbk.)

Introduction:

There is no doubt that quitting smoking is one of the hardest things to accomplish.
I should know, on October 26th, 2014, I smoked my last cigarette ... forever!

I also knew that for me to be successful, I had to start the process of quitting long before my 'non-smoking target day' of Oct 26. In fact, I started ONE MONTH prior to that date by first examining my personal smoking habits.

When I really got down to it, most of my nicotine cravings came from my daily smoking habits. Once I identified and understood those smoking habits that triggered my urges to smoke, I was able to break each habit one by one, making it easier to quit long before I actually started quitting. Identifying and admitting those nasty trigger habits was the first step in stopping the craving cycle and addiction.

For ONE MONTH I examined and recorded where, when and why I was smoking. I also recorded what or who was an outside influence on my cigarette consumption.

- Friends that smoked with me. Nothing is as good as hanging out with my girlfriends, having a cigarette or ten while we got caught up on our daily lives over a cup a coffee.
- A night out for drinks. I can openly admit alcohol and smoking cigarettes was probably my hardest challenge.
- Then there were those times of great anxiety in my life. Waiting for bad news ... or even good news. As long as there was some type of tension, I chained smoked to "calm my nerves."

Sound familiar? That's because these are real-life situations smokers often face in our lives.

For me, there were two specific everyday events that triggered my smoking cravings. Waiting for my car to 'warm up' in the wintertime, and having that final cigarette before going upstairs into my place in the Smoke-Free apartment building I lived in.

To this day, waiting while warming a car up in the wintertime makes my whole body crave a cigarette. Except now I have trained my mind to identify and override that craving. And you can accomplish this as well, through identifying your own trigger habits.

When I was a smoker, I detested people who offered advice about what method I should use to quit smoking. So, in turn, I will not give you any advice either.

Not one hint, not one rule. Nothing.

Right now, you're thinking, but this is a book about quitting smoking.

No, this is NOT a book about quitting smoking.

Wait ... WHAT?

This is a book, through tracking your daily smoking habits, allows you to identify and change your life habits so you no longer initiate your cravings for nicotine. Once you change your daily habits, the urges go away and so does your dependency on nicotine.

Here's an example of how I changed my habits and defeated my enemy ... my nicotine dependency.

Like many smokers, I enjoyed having a cigarette or five with my coffee while sitting outside with the other smokers of the building. In the designated smoking area. I always sat in the same chair on the same side of the building. I could feel my body craving nicotine even before I reached the chair outside. That craving was well ingrained in my mind and body, making it one of the habits I needed to break.

By identifying the situations as a trigger habit, I changed my lifestyle to avoid that craving. Instead of sitting in the same chair on the same side of the building, I changed that habit by enjoying my coffee in another location without smoking a cigarette. It was not easy at first, but eventually my mind and body associated my new location as a place I no longer smoked. Two months later, I could sit back in the same chair at the original location and be able to fend off my cravings for a cigarette even though I was sitting amongst the same smokers.

Sounds easy, right?
OH HELL, NO!
IT IS NOT EASY.
IT HARD ... REALLY, REALLY HARD.
BUT IF YOU TRULY WANT TO QUIT, YOU CAN DO IT JUST AS I DID.

I need to make it clear that I am NOT a medical professional.
I'm just an ordinary human just like you.
And If I can quit smoking, so can you.

I also need to point out, I can't guarantee that you will succeed in quitting smoking.

Your success is up to you.

Like me, if you are truly ready to never smoke again, then you will work hard to make that happen. But before you can butt out your last cigarette or tossed that last package of cigarettes in the garbage, you need to understand your habits.

You must know your enemy in order to defeat it.

The following book contains 31 days of blank forms for you to record your daily smoking activities BEFORE your targeted Non-smoking day.

Say your target date for Non-smoking starts on the first day of April. You would begin to fill out the forms with your habits 31 days BEFORE the first day of April, which is the first day of March.

Section One asks you to record the where, when, why, and how many cigarettes you consumed that day.

Section Two is for you to write down your own solutions for altering your life so you are no longer repeating that same habit when you do begin to quit and after your target date.

At the end of each 7 days, there is one quick self-analytical question used both to encourage and bolster your success in the future. These questions help you by changing your mindset, encouraging you to do better when you finally start quitting smoking.

The method is simple.

1. Identify your smoking habits.
2. Understand WHY you have that trigger habit.
3. Create a solution to that trigger habit that fits your life.
4. After ONE MONTH of knowing your enemy, you can begin to defeat it.

As I said before ... if I can do it ...

YOU CAN DO IT!!

WEEK ONE

Be truthful with yourself.
Be honest with yourself.
But most of all ...
Be kind to yourself.

SECTION ONE

Day: **Month:** **Year:** **DAY #:**

Where was I when the urge came?

What time of day?

What was I doing?

WHY did I smoke?

Who or what was an outside influence?

Number of cigarettes smoked in what length of time?

Location:	Time:	Total

SECTION TWO

MY HABIT BREAKING SOLUTION:

SECTION ONE

Day: **Month:** **Year:** **DAY #:**

Where was I when the urge came?

What time of day?

What was I doing?

WHY did I smoke?

Who or what was an outside influence?

Number of cigarettes smoked in what length of time?

Location:	Time:	Total

SECTION TWO

MY HABIT BREAKING SOLUTION:

SECTION ONE

Day: **Month:** **Year:** **DAY #:**

Where was I when the urge came?

What time of day?

What was I doing?

WHY did I smoke?

Who or what was an outside influence?

Number of cigarettes smoked in what length of time?

Location:	Time:	Total

SECTION TWO

MY HABIT BREAKING SOLUTION:

SECTION ONE

Day: **Month:** **Year:** **DAY #:**

Where was I when the urge came?

What time of day?

What was I doing?

WHY did I smoke?

Who or what was an outside influence?

Number of cigarettes smoked in what length of time?

Location:	Time:	Total

SECTION TWO

MY HABIT BREAKING SOLUTION:

SECTION ONE

Day: **Month:** **Year:** **DAY #:**

Where was I when the urge came?

What time of day?

What was I doing?

WHY did I smoke?

Who or what was an outside influence?

Number of cigarettes smoked in what length of time?

Location:	Time:	Total

SECTION TWO

MY HABIT BREAKING SOLUTION:

SECTION ONE

Day: **Month:** **Year:** **DAY #:**

Where was I when the urge came?

What time of day?

What was I doing?

WHY did I smoke?

Who or what was an outside influence?

Number of cigarettes smoked in what length of time?

Location:	Time:	Total

SECTION TWO

MY HABIT BREAKING SOLUTION:

SECTION ONE

Day: Month: Year: DAY #:

Where was I when the urge came?

What time of day?

What was I doing?

WHY did I smoke?

Who or what was an outside influence?

Number of cigarettes smoked in what length of time?

Location:	Time:	Total

SECTION TWO

MY HABIT BREAKING SOLUTION:

CONGRATULATIONS!

You have completed 7 days of self-analysis
on your own smoking habits.

Here's a motivator to help you keep going.

List 10 things you will reward yourself with
when you are no longer spending money on cigarettes?

1 ______________________________

2 ______________________________

3 ______________________________

4 ______________________________

5 ______________________________

6 ______________________________

7 ______________________________

8 ______________________________

9 ______________________________

10 ______________________________

WEEK TWO

SECTION ONE

Day: Month: Year: DAY #:

Where was I when the urge came?

What time of day?

What was I doing?

WHY did I smoke?

Who or what was an outside influence?

Number of cigarettes smoked in what length of time?

Location:	Time:	Total

SECTION TWO

MY HABIT BREAKING SOLUTION:

SECTION ONE

Day: **Month:** **Year:** **DAY #:**

Where was I when the urge came?

What time of day?

What was I doing?

WHY did I smoke?

Who or what was an outside influence?

Number of cigarettes smoked in what length of time?

Location:	Time:	Total

SECTION TWO

MY HABIT BREAKING SOLUTION:

SECTION ONE

Day: **Month:** **Year:** **DAY #:**

Where was I when the urge came?

What time of day?

What was I doing?

WHY did I smoke?

Who or what was an outside influence?

Number of cigarettes smoked in what length of time?

Location:	Time:	Total

SECTION TWO

MY HABIT BREAKING SOLUTION:

SECTION ONE

Day: Month: Year: DAY #:

Where was I when the urge came?

What time of day?

What was I doing?

WHY did I smoke?

Who or what was an outside influence?

Number of cigarettes smoked in what length of time?

Location:	Time:	Total

SECTION TWO

MY HABIT BREAKING SOLUTION:

SECTION ONE

Day: **Month:** **Year:** **DAY #:**

Where was I when the urge came?

What time of day?

What was I doing?

WHY did I smoke?

Who or what was an outside influence?

Number of cigarettes smoked in what length of time?

Location:	Time:	Total

SECTION TWO

MY HABIT BREAKING SOLUTION:

SECTION ONE

Day: Month: Year: DAY #:

Where was I when the urge came?

What time of day?

What was I doing?

WHY did I smoke?

Who or what was an outside influence?

Number of cigarettes smoked in what length of time?

Location:	Time:	Total

SECTION TWO

MY HABIT BREAKING SOLUTION:

SECTION ONE

Day: Month: Year: DAY #:

Where was I when the urge came?

What time of day?

What was I doing?

WHY did I smoke?

Who or what was an outside influence?

Number of cigarettes smoked in what length of time?

Location:	Time:	Total

SECTION TWO

MY HABIT BREAKING SOLUTION:

CONGRATULATIONS!

You have completed 14 days of self-analysis on your own smoking habits.

Here's more inspiration to help you keep going.

List 10 things you want do with the TIME you will have when you no longer smoke.

1 ____

2 ____

3 ____

4 ____

5 ____

6 ____

7 ____

8 ____

9 ____

10 ____

WEEK THREE

SECTION ONE

Day: **Month:** **Year:** **DAY #:**

Where was I when the urge came?

What time of day?

What was I doing?

WHY did I smoke?

Who or what was an outside influence?

Number of cigarettes smoked in what length of time?

Location:	Time:	Total

SECTION TWO

MY HABIT BREAKING SOLUTION:

SECTION ONE

Day: Month: Year: DAY #:

Where was I when the urge came?

What time of day?

What was I doing?

WHY did I smoke?

Who or what was an outside influence?

Number of cigarettes smoked in what length of time?

Location:	Time:	Total

SECTION TWO

MY HABIT BREAKING SOLUTION:

SECTION ONE

Day: Month: Year: DAY #:

Where was I when the urge came?

What time of day?

What was I doing?

WHY did I smoke?

Who or what was an outside influence?

Number of cigarettes smoked in what length of time?

Location:	Time:	Total

SECTION TWO

MY HABIT BREAKING SOLUTION:

SECTION ONE

Day: **Month:** **Year:** **DAY #:**

Where was I when the urge came?

What time of day?

What was I doing?

WHY did I smoke?

Who or what was an outside influence?

Number of cigarettes smoked in what length of time?

Location:	Time:	Total

SECTION TWO

MY HABIT BREAKING SOLUTION:

SECTION ONE

Day: Month: Year: DAY #:

Where was I when the urge came?

What time of day?

What was I doing?

WHY did I smoke?

Who or what was an outside influence?

Number of cigarettes smoked in what length of time?

Location:	Time:	Total

SECTION TWO

MY HABIT BREAKING SOLUTION:

SECTION ONE

Day: **Month:** **Year:** **DAY #:**

Where was I when the urge came?

What time of day?

What was I doing?

WHY did I smoke?

Who or what was an outside influence?

Number of cigarettes smoked in what length of time?

Location:	Time:	Total

SECTION TWO

MY HABIT BREAKING SOLUTION:

SECTION ONE

Day: Month: Year: DAY #:

Where was I when the urge came?

What time of day?

What was I doing?

WHY did I smoke?

Who or what was an outside influence?

Number of cigarettes smoked in what length of time?

Location:	Time:	Total

SECTION TWO

MY HABIT BREAKING SOLUTION:

CONGRATULATIONS!

You have completed 21 days of self-analysis on your own smoking habits.

Here's more encouragements to help you keep going.

List 10 HEALTH BENEFITS you will have when you no longer smoke cigarettes.

1 ____________________

2 ____________________

3 ____________________

4 ____________________

5 ____________________

6 ____________________

7 ____________________

8 ____________________

9 ____________________

10 ____________________

WEEK FOUR

SECTION ONE

Day: **Month:** **Year:** **DAY #:**

Where was I when the urge came?

What time of day?

What was I doing?

WHY did I smoke?

Who or what was an outside influence?

Number of cigarettes smoked in what length of time?

Location:	Time:	Total

SECTION TWO

MY HABIT BREAKING SOLUTION:

SECTION ONE

Day: Month: Year: DAY #:

Where was I when the urge came?

What time of day?

What was I doing?

WHY did I smoke?

Who or what was an outside influence?

Number of cigarettes smoked in what length of time?

Location:	Time:	Total

SECTION TWO

MY HABIT BREAKING SOLUTION:

SECTION ONE

Day: **Month:** **Year:** **DAY #:**

Where was I when the urge came?

What time of day?

What was I doing?

WHY did I smoke?

Who or what was an outside influence?

Number of cigarettes smoked in what length of time?

Location:	Time:	Total

SECTION TWO

MY HABIT BREAKING SOLUTION:

SECTION ONE

Day: **Month:** **Year:** **DAY #:**

Where was I when the urge came?

What time of day?

What was I doing?

WHY did I smoke?

Who or what was an outside influence?

Number of cigarettes smoked in what length of time?

Location:	Time:	Total

SECTION TWO

MY HABIT BREAKING SOLUTION:

SECTION ONE

Day: **Month:** **Year:** **DAY #:**

Where was I when the urge came?

What time of day?

What was I doing?

WHY did I smoke?

Who or what was an outside influence?

Number of cigarettes smoked in what length of time?

Location:	Time:	Total

SECTION TWO

MY HABIT BREAKING SOLUTION:

SECTION ONE

Day: **Month:** **Year:** **DAY #:**

Where was I when the urge came?

What time of day?

What was I doing?

WHY did I smoke?

Who or what was an outside influence?

Number of cigarettes smoked in what length of time?

Location:	Time:	Total

SECTION TWO

MY HABIT BREAKING SOLUTION:

SECTION ONE

Day: **Month:** **Year:** **DAY #:**

Where was I when the urge came?

What time of day?

What was I doing?

WHY did I smoke?

Who or what was an outside influence?

Number of cigarettes smoked in what length of time?

Location:	Time:	Total

SECTION TWO

MY HABIT BREAKING SOLUTION:

CONGRATULATIONS!

You have completed 28 days of self-analysis
on your own smoking habits.

Here's more incentive to help
you keep going.

List 10 reasons why you need to stop smoking.
Be truly honest with yourself.

1 ______________________________

2 ______________________________

3 ______________________________

4 ______________________________

5 ______________________________

6 ______________________________

7 ______________________________

8 ______________________________

9 ______________________________

10 ______________________________

THREE MORE DAYS

SECTION ONE

Day: **Month:** **Year:** **DAY #:**

Where was I when the urge came?

What time of day?

What was I doing?

WHY did I smoke?

Who or what was an outside influence?

Number of cigarettes smoked in what length of time?

Location:	Time:	Total

SECTION TWO

MY HABIT BREAKING SOLUTION:

SECTION ONE

Day: Month: Year: DAY #:

Where was I when the urge came?

What time of day?

What was I doing?

WHY did I smoke?

Who or what was an outside influence?

Number of cigarettes smoked in what length of time?

Location:	Time:	Total

SECTION TWO

MY HABIT BREAKING SOLUTION:

SECTION ONE

Day: **Month:** **Year:** **DAY #:**

Where was I when the urge came?

What time of day?

What was I doing?

WHY did I smoke?

Who or what was an outside influence?

Number of cigarettes smoked in what length of time?

Location:	Time:	Total

SECTION TWO

MY HABIT BREAKING SOLUTION:

CONGRATULATIONS!

You have completed
1 FULL MONTH
of self-analysis on your own smoking habits.

Here's 10 more important reasons to help you stop smoking.

List 10 people in your life that would be happy that you will quiet smoking and live a longer life.

1 ________________________________

2 ________________________________

3 ________________________________

4 ________________________________

5 ________________________________

6 ________________________________

7 ________________________________

8 ________________________________

9 ________________________________

10 ________________________________

You now have both the information and solution about your own smoking habits that will enable you to change your smoking habits and override those cravings.

Good Luck and ...
Breath well.
Smell good.
Live long.

Extra Notes

Extra Notes

Extra Notes

www.ingramcontent.com/pod-product-compliance
Lightning Source LLC
LaVergne TN
LVHW010941110826
845149LV00013B/2703

* 9 7 8 1 9 8 9 1 9 4 9 5 9 *